MARIA DE FATIMA CAMPOS was born in Brazil, and has exhibited in both Brazil and London.
She specialises in all things Brazilian: the landscapes, the lifestyle and the peoples.
Most recently, she held a one woman show – a celebration of her work from 1986-1996 –
at the Museum of Image and Sound in São Paulo.

Maria runs photographic workshops for both children and professional photographers,
and acts as consultant to a manufacturer of photographic materials in London. In 1995,
she was elected Associate of the Royal Photographic Society.

When she is not travelling in Brazil, Maria lives in Muswell Hill in North London.
This is her first book for Frances Lincoln.

I would like to dedicate this book to the memory of my mother who understood
my world of fantasy and my different attitudes towards life when I was a child, and also to all the children
around the world, hoping that they will have a better life in the future.

First published in Great Britain in 1999 by Frances Lincoln Children's Books, 4 Torriano Mews,
Torriano Avenue, London NW5 2RZ

www.franceslincoln.com

First published in paperback in 2000

Distributed in the USA by Publishers Group West

British Library Cataloguing in Publication Data available on request

ISBN 0-7112-1479-4 (UK)
ISBN 1-84507-316-9 (USA)

Set in Hiroshige Book
Printed in China

3 5 7 9 8 6 4

Acknowledgements
Special thanks to the following people and institutions for helping to make this book possible:
Maria Isabel Barbosa; my husband Richard Davis and Mrs Lilian Davis; Sra Yone and Dr José; Mauro and Elizabeth;
Sr Daniel Fresnot, Sr Helio do Espírito-Santo and Sr Vitor Peruari; Abadá Grupo de Capoeira;
Brazilian Embassy (Cultural and Information Departments); Casa Taiguara; Centro de Preservação da Arte,
Cultura e Ciências Indígenas; CTG Vinte de Setembro; EMBRAER; EMBRAPA; INPA; Laboratório Nacional de Luz Síncroton;
Oficina Santa Ana, Vila Prudente; Xavantes Indian Tribe from Mato Grosso, West Central Brazil.

B is for Brazil

Maria de Fatima Campos

FRANCES LINCOLN CHILDREN'S BOOKS

AUTHOR'S NOTE

As a photographer, I try to capture in my pictures the spirit of Brazil and what it means to me. Although these days I live mostly in London, I was born in Londrina (which means little London), in the south of Brazil, and I often go back home to take photographs and find out more about my country and people.

Brazil is a very special place to live because it is home to a mix of races – South American Indian, African and European. You can see these influences in the different clothes, foods, customs, religions and beliefs you come across wherever you go in Brazil. There's a variety of Brazilian languages too: the official language is Portuguese, but there are more than a hundred known Indian languages, and many others which haven't been written down and given names yet.

Brazil is a young country and there are many things to be done, but it is full of potential: we Brazilians believe that Brazil is the country of the future. I hope my ABC gives you an idea of what a colourful and exciting place it is, and what life is like for the people who live there.

Brazil

Aa

is for Amazon rain forest, the largest one in the world. The millions of trees that grow here are very important as they help control the world's climate and keep the air clean for us to breathe – the rain forests of Brazil are sometimes called 'the lungs of the world'.

 is for Brazil, a vast country which takes up almost half of the South American continent. It is full of contrasts, from the tropical rain forests of the north to modern cities like this one: Rio de Janeiro, where millions of people live and work.

is for Carnival. For three days in February, all of Brazil takes to the streets to celebrate. The carnival parade in Rio de Janeiro is famous all over the world. Carnival-goers spend months beforehand planning their costumes, decorating special parade floats and practising the samba – the traditional carnival dance.

Dd

is for Dancing capoeira, a ritualised form of self-defense. Performances are accompanied by the berimbau, a one-stringed instrument made from wood and gourd fruit. Capoeira was originally brought by slaves from Africa to the north-east of Brazil, but nowadays it is performed all over the country.

Ee is for Erva Mate, a herbal tea, traditionally drunk from a hollowed-out gourd fruit, like the one this gaúcho (cowgirl) from southern Brazil is holding. When the fruit is ripe, it is emptied, decorated with gold and silver and then used as a cup. The tea is drunk through a metal pipe.

Ff

is for Football, Brazil's national sport. People play anywhere they can – out in the streets, by the sea, or in the parks near their homes.

Gg

is for Guaraná, the seed of the guaranazeiro tree which grows only in the Amazon rain forest. It is used as a medicine for heart diseases and as an all-round tonic. The Maue – a local Indian tribe – drink guaraná juice to cure illness and bring good luck.

 is for House on stilts. Houses near the River Amazon are built on stilts because in the rainy season, from January to June, it rains nearly every day and the land is flooded. When this happens, people have to leave their front door by boat!

 is for Iguaçú Falls, which means Great Falls. Iguaçú is the largest waterfall in the world, and its power is used to supply the world's biggest hydroelectric plant.

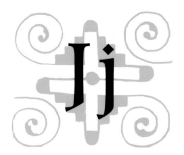

Jj

is for Jangada, a small fishing boat
used in the north-east of Brazil,
on the Atlantic Ocean. It has a
triangular sail, a paddle, and
a seat for the fisherman.

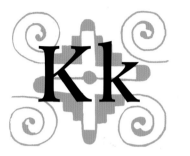 **Kk** is for the Kisses we give to our family and friends. Brazilians say hello or goodbye with one, two or even three kisses. It is said that if you are single and give someone three kisses, you will soon be married!

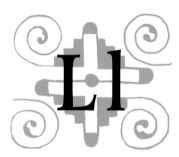 **Ll** is for Learning. Children in Brazil go to school at seven in the morning and come home by lunchtime. After lunch, they can attend special classes like ballet or capoeira, or go to workshops to learn skills which will help them get a job when they leave school. This boy is learning about electricity.

 is for Market where people can buy all kinds of delicious fruits and vegetables. Everything is grown locally so it is always fresh. Shoppers like to pick and choose for themselves to make sure they get the best.

Nn

is for the Net, usually homemade, which is used to catch fish. On the rivers, children often fish from a canoe with a small net. Fisherman at the coast have such large nets that it can take sixty people to pull one in when it is full of fish.

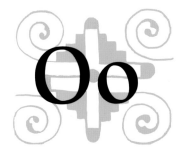

Oo

is for Oranges, which grow all over Brazil. You can buy fresh orange juice from machines which squeeze the oranges in front of you while you wait.

Pp

is for Painting. In Curitiba in the south of Brazil, the council runs a painting project for children on Saturday mornings. They provide hundreds of metres of paper, lots of paints and brushes, and any child who is passing can have a go.

Qq is for eQuator, the imaginary circle which runs around the earth, halfway between the North and South poles. Countries on the equator receive more of the sun's energy than anywhere else on our planet. The equator runs right through Brazil's rain forests, so they are very fertile and full of many different plants and animals.

Rr

is for Rubber, made from a liquid called latex which is milked from the bark of the rubber tree. This tree is native to the Amazon rain forest, and nowadays there are lots of rubber tree plantations in the south-east of Brazil. The rubber is sent to factories to be made into tyres for cars.

is for Spice. Everyone in Brazil uses spice to add flavour and colour to their cooking, but the people in the north-east of Brazil are particularly fond of spicy food. They add spice – especially chilli peppers and paprika – to almost everything. Sometimes the food is so hot, they say their ears and eyes will catch fire.

Tt

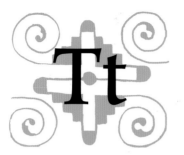

is for Technology. Brazil has a very large aircraft industry, producing planes like this passenger jet. The three engineers here are making sure that everything is working properly.

Uu

is for Urucum, originally used by the Brazilian Indians as a dye to paint their bodies, clothes and utensils. The urucum tree has beautiful pale pink flowers. A powder made from its crushed seeds is used as a food colouring.

is for Voyage. Because Brazil is so large, people are used to making long voyages. In some areas of the Amazon, the easiest and most comfortable way to travel is by boat. People take hammocks and sit on deck to keep cool and watch the scenery.

 is for Water. These Indian children in Mato Grosso play in the lake every day. When an Indian mother is about to have a baby, she goes to her local river and gives birth in the water. Maybe that is why these children love playing in water so much.

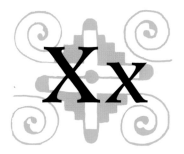

Xx

is for the Xavantes Indian tribe, from Cerrados in the central-west part of Brazil. The Xavantes make straw baskets like these for women to carry their babies on their backs. The baskets are called *tsiõnõ* in Xavantes language, which means 'motherly protection'.

is for Yellow, Green and Blue, the three colours of the Brazilian flag. The yellow is for the gold and other metals and precious stones found all over Brazil; the green is for the rain forests; and the blue is for Brazil's bright blue skies. The words written in the white band mean 'order and progress'.

 is for Zebu cattle which were brought to Brazil from India. The cowboy here is holding an instrument called a berrante, made from cattle horns. Berrantes make a deep mooing sound. Cow herds use them to round up zebu when they need to move them to a new field.

W is for World

Kathryn Cave
In Association with Oxfam

This round-the-world alphabet covers more than twenty countries,
from Greenland to Vietnam. Heart-warming photography from Oxfam and simple text
by award-winning author Kathryn Cave make it an alphabet book with a difference:
a step on the path towards learning and an introduction
to the challenging world we share.

I is for India

Prodeepta Das

From Bullock cart to Peacock, from Namaskar to Tea,
here is a celebration of India in all its colourful diversity. In this photographic alphabet,
Prodeepta Das introduces young readers to some of the customs, religions and forms of culture –
both ancient and modern – that can be found all over India.

C is for China

Sungwan So

From Abacus to Lantern, from Jade to Wenzi,
this photographic alphabet introduces young readers to the rich culture and natural beauty of China.
Sungwan So's colourful variety of images are a tribute to a traditional society whose people
have faced the challenges of revolutionary change with courage and strength.

Frances Lincoln titles are available from all good bookshops.
You can also buy books and find out more about your favourite titles, authors and illustrators
on our website: www.franceslincoln.com

OCT 11 2006